Pet Isopods: The

Keeping and Caring for Your Tiny

Crustacean Friends

Dr. Gerard Benjamin Phillips

Copyright and Disclaimer

Table of Contents

Introduction

Welcome to the captivating universe of Pet Isopods! In this extensive guide, we will embark on a profound exploration, delving into the nuanced intricacies of keeping and caring for these remarkable crustaceans as your delightful and low-maintenance companions.

Understanding Isopods

What are Isopods?

Isopods, belonging to the order Isopoda within the class Malacostraca, form an intriguing branch of the crustacean family. These small, segmented creatures, with over 10,000 recognized species, demonstrate remarkable diversity in size, color, and behavior. While sharing a distant kinship with marine arthropods like lobsters and crabs, isopods have successfully adapted to terrestrial life, showcasing an evolutionary marvel that sets them apart.

The Fascinating World of Crustaceans

Within the realm of crustaceans, isopods play a distinctive role. Known for their ability to thrive in various environments, from terrestrial to aquatic, these creatures contribute significantly to ecosystems. Their evolution to terrestrial life presents a captivating narrative of adaptation and survival.

Why Choose Isopods as Pets?

Isopods, as pets, offer a unique and rewarding experience for enthusiasts. Their gentle nature, intriguing behaviors, and relatively straightforward care requirements make them an ideal choice for both novice and experienced pet owners. Throughout this guide, we will delve into the specifics of selecting, housing, feeding, and caring for your isopod companions, ensuring a comprehensive understanding of these tiny crustacean friends.

Now that we have laid a foundation by introducing the basics, let's progress to Chapter 1, where we will explore the diverse world of isopod species, guiding you in choosing the perfect companions tailored to your preferences and environment.

Chapter 1: Selecting the Right Isopod Species

Embark on the exciting journey of selecting the right isopod species as we dive into the diverse and fascinating realm of these tiny crustacean companions. This chapter serves as your comprehensive guide, unraveling the unique characteristics of popular isopod species for pets and providing essential considerations for making informed choices that align with your preferences and the well-being of your isopods.

Popular Isopod Species for Pets: An In-Depth Exploration

Armadillidium spp.: Unveiling the Charismatic "Roly-Polies"

Overview: Armadillidium, commonly known as "roly-polies" or "pillbugs," emerge as enchanting isopod companions renowned for their endearing ability to roll into a protective ball when threatened. This distinctive behavior, coupled with a diverse array of colors and patterns, not only adds aesthetic allure but also introduces a touch of charm to your isopod collection.

Unique Characteristics: Armadillidium species exhibit a remarkable range of characteristics, making them stand out in the world of isopods. Their ability to roll into a ball serves as a distinctive defense mechanism, contributing significantly to their widespread popularity. This behavior not only captivates observers but also provides an extra layer of protection for the isopods against potential threats.

The fascination doesn't end there – the Armadillidium genus showcases an impressive diversity of color morphs and patterns. From earthy tones that mimic their natural habitats to vibrant hues that showcase the beauty of biodiversity, enthusiasts have the privilege of selecting from a visually diverse and appealing array for their isopod collections. The variety within the Armadillidium genus makes them particularly sought after among hobbyists seeking a visually striking and engaging addition to their vivariums.

Habitat Preferences: Understanding the habitat preferences of Armadillidium species is crucial for creating an environment where they can thrive. These isopods, hailing from regions with moderate to high humidity, are ideally suited for vivariums that replicate their natural conditions. Consider the following aspects when setting up a habitat for Armadillidium spp.:

1. **Moist Environments:** Armadillidium species thrive in moist environments. Ensure the substrate retains moisture well, using materials like coconut coir or a mix of soil and leaf litter.

2. **Higher Humidity Levels:** Vivariums for Armadillidium should maintain higher humidity levels to mimic their natural habitats. Regular misting and providing a source of humidity, such as a water dish, contribute to their overall well-being.

3. **Hideouts and Substrate Depth:** Armadillidium spp. appreciate hiding places and substrate depth that allows for burrowing. Providing ample hiding spots encourages natural behaviors and reduces stress.

Creating a vivarium that mirrors the natural conditions of Armadillidium species enhances their overall health and allows enthusiasts to observe their unique behaviors in a setting that closely resembles their native habitats.

Conclusion: Armadillidium spp., the charismatic "roly-polies," bring a delightful blend of captivating behaviors and visually stunning characteristics to the world of isopod enthusiasts. From their endearing ability to roll into protective balls to the diverse palette of colors and patterns within the genus, these isopods offer a unique and engaging experience for hobbyists. Understanding their habitat preferences is crucial for creating a thriving environment where Armadillidium species can express their natural behaviors. By providing optimal conditions, enthusiasts can cultivate a vibrant and dynamic setup that showcases the charm of these fascinating isopods.

Porcellio spp.: Embracing the Versatility of "Woodlice"

Overview: Porcellio isopods, commonly known as "woodlice" or "sowbugs," distinguish themselves with their robust hardiness and exceptional adaptability. Renowned for their captivating spectrum of colors and their role as proficient cleaners within enclosures, Porcellio isopods stand as a valuable addition to isopod communities

Unique Characteristics: Porcellio isopods exhibit a remarkable spectrum of colors, ranging from subtle earth tones to striking shades, adding an aesthetic dimension to their appeal. This diversity in coloration contributes to their popularity among isopod enthusiasts, allowing hobbyists to select from a visually appealing range when curating their collections.

One of the key features that make Porcellio isopods stand out is their robust hardiness. These isopods showcase an exceptional ability to thrive in diverse environments, making them an excellent choice for hobbyists seeking resilient and adaptable additions to their setups. Their hardiness extends to their resistance to environmental fluctuations, making them well-suited for various vivarium conditions.

Versatility in Setups: Porcellio species exhibit remarkable versatility, adapting well to different enclosure types. Whether incorporated into bioactive terrariums, paludariums, or kept in simpler pet containers, Porcellio isopods actively contribute to the decomposition of organic matter. Their role as efficient cleaners aids in maintaining a healthy and balanced ecosystem within the enclosure.

For bioactive setups, Porcellio isopods play a crucial role in waste decomposition, assisting in breaking down organic matter and contributing to nutrient cycling. In simpler pet containers, they offer enthusiasts a low-maintenance yet visually engaging option for observing isopod behavior and natural interactions.

Habitat Preferences: Porcellio species generally prefer moderately humid environments. When creating a habitat for Porcellio isopods, consider the following factors:

1. **Substrate:** Provide a substrate that retains moisture well, such as coconut coir or a mix of soil and leaf litter, offering ample hiding places.

2. **Humidity Levels:** Maintain moderate humidity levels, achieved through regular misting and providing a water dish to meet their hydration needs.

3. **Hideouts:** Porcellio isopods appreciate hiding places, so include suitable materials like cork bark or pieces of wood to create natural shelters.

Conclusion: Porcellio spp., the versatile "woodlice," bring a combination of robust hardiness, captivating colors, and active cleaning behaviors to the world of isopod enthusiasts. Whether incorporated into elaborate bioactive setups or kept in simpler pet containers, Porcellio isopods contribute actively to the well-being of their enclosures. Understanding their habitat preferences and appreciating their adaptability allows enthusiasts to create thriving environments that showcase the versatility and charm of these remarkable isopods. Whether you are a seasoned hobbyist or a newcomer to isopod keeping, Porcellio isopods stand as a captivating and resilient choice for diverse enclosure setups.

Cubaris spp.: Embracing the Delightful "Dwarf Isopods"

Overview: Cubaris isopods, affectionately known as "dwarf isopods," captivate enthusiasts with their diminutive size and intricate patterns. Despite their small stature, Cubaris species exhibit social behaviors that make them delightful and engaging pets to observe. With a preference for humid environments, Cubaris isopods present a distinct choice for keepers seeking a balance between uniqueness and manageability in their isopod collection.

Unique Characteristics: Cubaris isopods are characterized by their diminutive size, making them a unique addition to the world of isopod keeping. Their small stature, typically ranging from a few millimeters to a centimeter, adds a charming element to their presence in captivity. Despite their size, Cubaris isopods exhibit intricate patterns that contribute to their visual appeal. The intricate patterns on their exoskeletons vary between species, offering enthusiasts a diverse selection to choose from for their isopod collections.

Their social behaviors further enhance their charm. Cubaris isopods often exhibit gregarious tendencies, displaying group activities and interactions that are captivating to observe. This communal aspect adds an extra layer of interest for enthusiasts who appreciate the dynamic behaviors of isopods.

Preference for Humid Environments: Cubaris isopods thrive in humid conditions, and understanding their habitat requirements is essential for their well-being. Here are key considerations when creating a habitat for Cubaris spp.:

1. **Substrate:** Provide a substrate that retains moisture well, such as a mix of sphagnum moss, coconut coir, and leaf litter. This ensures a suitable environment for burrowing and moisture retention.

2. **Humidity Levels:** Maintain consistently high humidity levels, ranging between 70-90%, to mimic their natural habitats. Regular misting and the inclusion of a water dish contribute to maintaining optimal humidity.

3. **Temperature:** Keep temperatures within a range of 70-80°F (21-27°C) to provide a comfortable and stable environment for Cubaris isopods.

4. **Hideouts:** Offer ample hiding places, such as cork bark or leaf litter, to accommodate their preference for sheltered spaces. This supports natural behaviors and reduces stress.

Understanding and replicating the natural conditions of humid environments is crucial for the well-being and thriving of Cubaris isopods.

Conclusion: Cubaris spp., the delightful "dwarf isopods," offer enthusiasts a unique and charming experience in isopod keeping. Their diminutive size, intricate patterns, and social behaviors make them a captivating choice for those seeking a balance between uniqueness and manageability in their isopod collections. Creating a habitat that aligns with their preference for humid environments ensures the optimal health and well-being of Cubaris isopods, allowing enthusiasts to enjoy the delightful presence of these charming dwarf isopods in their vivariums. Whether you are a seasoned isopod keeper or a newcomer to the hobby, Cubaris spp. stand as a delightful and intriguing addition to the diverse world of isopods.

As you embark on the isopod-keeping journey, the careful selection of the right species serves as the cornerstone for a harmonious and thriving habitat. In the upcoming chapter, we will delve into the intricacies of setting up the perfect isopod enclosure, providing practical insights and tips for creating a comfortable and enriching home for your tiny crustacean companions.

Chapter 2: Creating the Perfect Isopod Habitat

Setting up an ideal habitat for your pet isopods is a multifaceted and nuanced task that requires meticulous attention to detail. In this chapter, we will delve into the essential elements of creating the perfect isopod habitat, covering substrate selection, decor and hiding places, ventilation and humidity control, temperature and lighting requirements, and the crucial choice of enclosure size.

Substrate Selection: The Foundation of Isopod Well-being

The substrate forms the foundation of an isopod's environment, mirroring their natural habitat and supporting their vital activities. Thoughtful consideration of substrate components is essential to foster a thriving isopod community.

Organic Materials Composition: Isopods, as decomposers, flourish in an environment that replicates the organic composition of their natural surroundings. Optimal substrate blends include coconut coir, sphagnum moss, and leaf litter. These materials create a rich, textured base that allows for burrowing, foraging, and moisture retention, essential for maintaining the humidity levels required by isopods.

Depth and Structure: Ensuring an ample depth of substrate is crucial for promoting natural behaviors. Isopods, with their instinctive burrowing tendencies, benefit from having enough material to create tunnels and chambers. A substrate depth of at least several inches provides the necessary space for these activities, contributing to their overall well-being and sense of security.

Decor and Hiding Places: Enhancing Aesthetic Appeal and Functionality

Beyond the substrate, the inclusion of natural decor and hiding spots transforms the isopod enclosure into a dynamic and engaging environment. This not only adds aesthetic appeal but also serves functional purposes for the isopods.

Natural Elements: Incorporating natural elements like pieces of bark, cork bark flats, and various types of wood contributes to the isopod habitat's authenticity. These materials serve as both decorative elements and functional structures, offering hiding places and molting sites for the isopods. Their natural instincts are stimulated when provided with a variety of textures and surfaces to explore.

Texture and Diversity: Diversity in textures and hiding places caters to the varied needs of different isopod species. Some may prefer rough bark, while others may seek the shelter of cork flats. Providing a range of options allows isopods to exhibit their natural behaviors, promoting a more dynamic and enriching environment. Experimenting with different textures and observing your isopods' preferences adds an extra layer of engagement to the habitat design.

Ventilation and Humidity Control: Creating an Optimal Microclimate

Maintaining a healthy isopod environment involves careful management of ventilation and humidity. The specific needs may vary depending on the isopod species you are keeping.

Ventilation Features: Proper ventilation is paramount for preventing mold growth and ensuring a well-ventilated habitat. Mesh lids and side vents are effective features that facilitate optimal airflow. These features also aid in regulating temperature and preventing the enclosure from becoming stagnant. Ventilation is a balancing act, as too much can lead to excessive drying, while too little can result in high humidity levels.

Humidity Management: Isopods, originating from a multitude of environments, exhibit a broad spectrum of humidity preferences reflective of their diverse habitats. To ensure the well-being of your isopods, comprehensive humidity management is pivotal.

Understanding Isopod Humidity Preferences:

Isopods, hailing from diverse ecological origins, exhibit distinct humidity requirements that are crucial for their physiological functions and overall health. Keepers must familiarize themselves with the native habitats of specific isopod species, whether they originate from tropical rainforests, temperate woodlands, or arid regions. Armed with this knowledge, keepers can create environments that closely mimic the natural conditions, promoting the optimal well-being of their isopod community. In this comprehensive guide, we will explore the humidity preferences of three main isopod genera: Armadillidium, Porcellio, and Cubaris.

Armadillidium: Armadillidium isopods, known as "roly-polies," predominantly inhabit temperate woodlands. They thrive in environments with moderate humidity levels. When creating a habitat for Armadillidium spp., consider the following:

- **Substrate:** Provide a substrate that retains moisture well, such as a mix of soil, leaf litter, and coconut coir. This ensures a suitable environment for burrowing.

- **Humidity Levels:** Maintain humidity levels in the range of 50-70%. While they don't require extremely high humidity, providing a moist environment is essential for molting and overall health.

- **Ventilation:** Ensure proper ventilation to prevent excessive moisture buildup, which can lead to respiratory issues. Well-ventilated enclosures with a secure lid strike a balance for Armadillidium isopods.

Porcellio: Porcellio isopods, commonly referred to as "woodlice" or "sowbugs," showcase robust hardiness and adaptability. Their habitat preferences vary slightly among species, but a general guideline includes:

- **Substrate:** Utilize a mix of coconut coir, soil, and leaf litter for substrate composition. Porcellio spp. appreciate hiding places within the substrate.

- **Humidity Levels:** Maintain moderate to high humidity levels, typically ranging from 50-80%. Regular misting and a water dish contribute to the overall moisture content.

- **Hideouts:** Provide hiding places such as cork bark or pieces of wood to accommodate their preference for sheltered spaces.

Cubaris: Cubaris isopods, known as "dwarf isopods," are characterized by their diminutive size and intricate patterns. They prefer humid environments similar to tropical rainforests. Consider the following for their care:

- **Substrate:** Use a mix of sphagnum moss, coconut coir, and leaf litter to create a substrate that retains moisture well. Cubaris spp. benefit from burrowing.

- **Humidity Levels:** Maintain consistently high humidity levels, ideally ranging from 70-90%. Regular misting and a water dish are essential components of their habitat.

By tailoring the habitat conditions to the specific humidity preferences of Armadillidium, Porcellio, and Cubaris isopods, keepers can ensure the well-being of their isopod communities. This nuanced approach enhances the overall health, reproductive success, and natural behaviors of these fascinating crustaceans. Additionally, it allows enthusiasts to create vivariums that accurately reflect the ecological niches from which these isopod species originate, fostering a more authentic and enjoyable isopod-keeping experience.

Regular Misting Practices: One effective method to meet the humidity needs of your isopods is through regular misting of the enclosure. This practice is particularly beneficial in areas with lower ventilation, where moisture retention might be challenging. Misting helps create a microclimate within the enclosure, providing the necessary moisture for isopods to engage in natural behaviors, facilitate molting, and maintain overall hydration levels. The frequency of misting should be adjusted based on the specific requirements of your isopod species and the prevailing environmental conditions.

Monitoring with Precision: Utilizing a hygrometer becomes an invaluable tool in the keeper's arsenal for precise humidity management. A hygrometer allows you to quantitatively measure the humidity levels within the enclosure, offering insights into whether the existing conditions align with the needs of your isopod species. Regular monitoring ensures that adjustments can be made promptly, preventing potential issues associated with excessive dryness or excessive humidity. This hands-on approach empowers keepers to create a stable microclimate that mirrors the ideal conditions for their isopods' thriving health.

Adjusting Ventilation for Stability: Ventilation plays a pivotal role in humidity regulation within the isopod enclosure. Depending on the species and their specific requirements, ventilation features such as mesh lids and side vents should be strategically utilized. Monitoring the humidity levels and adjusting ventilation accordingly allows keepers to strike a delicate balance, preventing the development of excessive moisture that can lead to mold growth or, conversely, ensuring sufficient humidity for isopods that thrive in moister environments. This dynamic approach to ventilation management contributes significantly to the creation of a stable and healthy microenvironment for your isopod community.

Temperature and Lighting Requirements: Regulating the Habitat Environment

Isopods, as ectothermic creatures, rely on their environment to regulate their body temperature. Maintaining appropriate temperature and lighting conditions is crucial for their metabolic functions and overall well-being.

Temperature Stability: Isopods thrive within a stable temperature range typically between 70°F and 80°F (21°C and 27°C). Fluctuations outside this range can impact their activity levels, reproduction, and overall health. Monitoring the ambient temperature and providing a consistent environment supports their metabolic processes and encourages normal behaviors.

Lighting for Observation: While isopods are generally nocturnal, providing ambient lighting in the enclosure aids in observation and maintaining a natural day-night cycle. Low-intensity lighting, such as LED strips, simulates moonlight and allows keepers to observe their isopods without causing stress or disruption to their natural behavior patterns.

Choosing the Right Enclosure Size: Providing Space for Exploration and Well-being

Selecting an enclosure of the appropriate size is a critical decision that directly influences the isopods' behavior, activity levels, and overall health. Adequate space allows for natural behaviors and contributes to a harmonious colony.

Considerations for Size: Choosing an enclosure size that accommodates the specific needs and behaviors of your selected isopod species is paramount. A larger enclosure not only provides more space for exploration but also allows for the inclusion of multiple hiding spots, contributing to the overall well-being of the colony. As isopods are communal creatures, providing ample space reduces stress and territorial disputes.

Population Growth Considerations: When determining the size of the enclosure, it's crucial to consider the potential growth of your isopod population. Overcrowding can lead to increased competition for resources and potential stress-related issues. A well-planned enclosure size accounts for both the current and future needs of your isopod community.

In conclusion, the successful setup of an isopod habitat involves a thoughtful blend of substrate selection, decor arrangement, ventilation and humidity control, temperature regulation, and choosing the right enclosure size. These elements collectively contribute to the health and vitality of your isopod companions. As you embark on this journey, consider each facet as an integral part of creating a thriving environment for these fascinating crustaceans. In Chapter 3, we will explore the crucial aspect of feeding and nutrition, ensuring your isopods receive a balanced and wholesome diet for optimal health.

Chapter 3: Feeding and Nutrition

Isopods, commonly known as woodlice or pill bugs, are fascinating creatures that have gained popularity as pets due to their unique characteristics and low-maintenance care. While isopods are often found in terrestrial environments, providing a suitable diet is crucial to ensure their health and well-being.

Basic Dietary Requirements: Isopods are detritivores, meaning they primarily feed on decaying organic matter. In captivity, replicating their natural diet is essential for their optimal health. Commonly accepted foods for pet isopods include leaf litter, rotting wood, and decomposing plant material. These items not only serve as a food source but also provide essential nutrients and fiber.

What to Feed:

- **Leaf Litter:** Fallen leaves from deciduous trees such as oak, maple, and beech are ideal. These leaves break down slowly, providing a continuous food source.

- **Decomposing Wood:** Isopods benefit from chewing on rotting wood or bark, obtaining nutrients during the decomposition process.

- **Vegetable Scraps:** Foods like carrots, potatoes, and other non-citrus vegetables can be offered in small quantities.

- **Calcium-Rich Foods:** Provide sources of calcium, such as crushed eggshells or cuttlebone, to support the molting process and maintain exoskeleton strength.

Quantities and Frequencies:

- **Leaf Litter:** Offer a generous amount of leaf litter, enough to cover the enclosure floor. Replace it as it decomposes.

- **Decomposing Wood:** Introduce small pieces of rotting wood, ensuring they do not overwhelm the enclosure. Replace when necessary.

- **Vegetable Scraps:** Offer small portions of vegetables once or twice a week. Monitor consumption to avoid overfeeding.

- **Calcium-Rich Foods:** Provide a continuous source of calcium, either as a separate dish or scattered throughout the enclosure.

Feeding Method:

Isopods are opportunistic feeders, and their feeding method is simple. Scatter food evenly across the enclosure to allow them to forage naturally. Ensure that food items are appropriately sized for the isopods to consume easily. Regularly monitor the enclosure to remove any uneaten or moldy food to maintain a clean and hygienic environment.

Supplemental Foods and Supplements:

In addition to the primary diet, consider incorporating the following supplemental foods and supplements:

- **Fish Flakes or Fish Pellets:** These provide additional protein and can be offered occasionally.

- **Fruit:** Offer small amounts of non-acidic fruit, such as apple or pear, as a treat.

- **Commercial Isopod Food:** Specially formulated isopod food is available and can be used to supplement their diet. Follow the manufacturer's recommendations for usage.

Chapter 4: Reproduction and Life Cycle

Embarking on the captivating journey of isopod reproduction unveils a fascinating realm of life cycles, courtship rituals, and the delicate transition from eggs to juveniles. This chapter aims to provide a comprehensive understanding of isopod reproduction, offering insights into the mesmerizing intricacies that shape the continuation and expansion of your isopod colonies.

Understanding Isopod Reproduction: A Prelude to Life's Ballet

Isopods, with their unique reproductive strategies, contribute an extra layer of fascination to the realm of isopod keeping. A deep understanding of isopod reproduction is not just a theoretical endeavor but a practical necessity for those aspiring to maintain and potentially expand their isopod colonies. The reproductive journey of isopods unfolds as a ballet, with each species performing its unique dance in the intricate theater of nature.

Mating Behavior: The Mesmerizing Ballet of Courtship

The intricate world of isopod mating rituals is a sight to behold, a mesmerizing ballet choreographed by nature itself. Male isopods take center stage, initiating courtship displays to attract potential mates. These dances, often species-specific, involve a captivating blend of movement and signaling that goes beyond mere procreation. Observing these rituals in your isopod community is not just a scientific observation but a truly captivating aspect of keeping these tiny creatures.

The courtship dance varies among species, showcasing the diversity of nature's creativity. Some isopods may engage in intricate movements, while others rely on pheromones to signal their readiness to mate.

Egg Development and Hatching: The Delicate Threads of Life

As the courtship concludes, the next act in the isopod life cycle begins with the fertilization of eggs. The female isopod carries these fertilized eggs in a specialized pouch until they hatch into tiny juvenile isopods. This phase is delicate and critical, requiring careful attention to environmental conditions for the successful transition from egg to offspring.

Providing an optimal environment during egg development and hatching is paramount. Precise humidity levels and temperature contribute to the health and viability of the eggs. A well-maintained enclosure ensures the delicate threads of life woven into each egg have the best chance of thriving. The hatching process is a moment of anticipation, marking the beginning of the isopod's independent life.

Nurturing Isopod Offspring: A Symphony of Growth and Care

The arrival of juvenile isopods heralds a new chapter in the isopod keeper's journey. Nurturing these tiny offspring requires specific care to ensure their well-being and successful transition to mature isopods. Creating a supportive environment involves providing secure hiding places, a nutrient-rich diet, and attentive monitoring during crucial stages such as molting.

Enclosure Conditions: Creating a Haven for Growth

A secure environment is essential for the well-being of juvenile isopods. Ample hiding places, strategically placed within the enclosure, provide a sense of security for these tiny creatures. These hiding spots mimic the natural microhabitats isopods seek in the wild, fostering a stress-free environment that encourages exploration and growth.

Nutrient-Rich Diet: Fueling the Journey to Adulthood

Juvenile isopods require a diet rich in nutrients to support their rapid growth. Offering a variety of foods, including organic matter, fresh fruits, and vegetables, ensures they receive the essential nutrients for development. Calcium-rich sources, such as cuttlebone or crushed eggshells, contribute to the formation of sturdy exoskeletons during molting.

Monitoring During Molting: A Crucial Phase of Transition

Molting is a critical stage in the life of an isopod, where they shed their exoskeleton to accommodate their growing bodies. Regular monitoring during molting stages helps prevent potential issues. Providing a stress-free environment, maintaining proper humidity levels, and ensuring a calcium-rich diet contribute to a healthy transition from juveniles to mature isopods.

The Depth of Reproductive Understanding: A Journey Beyond Observation

Understanding the intricacies of isopod reproduction adds a layer of depth to the joy of isopod keeping. The unique courtship rituals, delicate egg development, and the nurturing care of offspring all contribute to the tapestry of life within your isopod colony. This chapter serves as a gateway to a deeper connection with these tiny crustacean companions.

In the upcoming chapter, we will delve into the nuanced aspects of maintaining the health of your isopods, recognizing signs of well-being, and addressing common health concerns. This knowledge is vital for providing a supportive environment for your isopod companions throughout their entire life cycle. As you navigate the enchanting world of isopod reproduction, may your understanding deepen, and your appreciation for these remarkable creatures grow.

Chapter 5: Health and Common Issues

Nurturing a thriving isopod community goes beyond providing a suitable habitat and balanced diet. Chapter 5 delves into the intricacies of health monitoring, recognizing signs of a healthy isopod, common health concerns, and establishing first aid and remedies. As a conscientious isopod keeper, understanding and addressing these aspects are crucial for the longevity and well-being of your tiny crustacean companions.

Recognizing Signs of a Healthy Isopod: The Art of Observation

The health of your isopods is a testament to your care and attention. Recognizing signs of a healthy isopod involves a nuanced understanding of their behaviors, physical appearance, and responsiveness to their environment.

Activity Levels: Vibrancy as a Sign of Well-being

Healthy isopods exhibit vibrant and active behaviors, engaging in natural activities such as foraging, exploring, and interacting with their surroundings. Regular observation allows you to establish a baseline for normal behavior within your specific isopod community. Deviations from this baseline, such as sudden lethargy or a decrease in activity, may indicate underlying health issues that warrant investigation.

Observing their interactions with each other and the environment provides insights into their social dynamics and environmental preferences. A healthy community will showcase a dynamic and lively atmosphere, enhancing the overall well-being of each individual isopod.

Exoskeleton Appearance: A Window into Molting Success

Molting is a pivotal aspect of an isopod's life cycle. A healthy molting process results in a smooth and complete shedding of the exoskeleton. The shed exoskeleton should appear intact, without deformities or abnormalities. Understanding the molting process and recognizing when it occurs contributes significantly to assessing the health of your isopods.

Regularly inspecting molted exoskeletons within the enclosure provides valuable insights into the molting success of your colony. A healthy molt is indicative of proper environmental conditions, a balanced diet, and overall well-being. Deviations, such as incomplete molts or abnormalities in exoskeleton appearance, may be early signs of underlying health concerns.

Responsiveness to Environment: Adaptability as a Health Indicator

Healthy isopods demonstrate an adaptive responsiveness to changes in their environment. They exhibit alertness and the ability to cope with variations in temperature, humidity, and other environmental factors. Understanding the baseline environmental needs of your specific isopod species aids in recognizing when adjustments are required.

Monitoring how your isopods respond to changes, whether in temperature or humidity levels, provides valuable feedback on their adaptability and resilience. An environment that supports their natural behaviors and responses contributes to their overall health and vitality.

Common Health Concerns: Addressing Challenges in Isopod Care

Despite their hardiness, isopods may encounter health challenges. Familiarizing yourself with common concerns allows for prompt identification and intervention, ensuring the well-being of your isopod colony.

Molting Issues: Navigating Challenges in Shedding

Molting problems can arise, leading to stuck exoskeletons or difficulties shedding. Maintaining proper humidity levels is crucial during the molting process, as it facilitates the shedding of the exoskeleton. Offering hiding spots and providing a calcium-rich diet can mitigate molting issues. Regularly inspecting molted exoskeletons in the enclosure provides valuable insights into the molting success of your colony.

Parasites and Infections: Vigilance for Well-being

Isopods, like any living organisms, may be susceptible to parasites or infections. Changes in behavior, lethargy, or abnormalities in appearance may signal underlying health issues. A proactive approach involves promptly isolating affected individuals to prevent the potential spread of parasites or infections throughout the colony.

Vigilance in monitoring your isopod community allows for early detection of potential health concerns. Regular health checks, visual inspections, and attentive observation contribute to the overall well-being of your isopods.

First Aid and Remedies: A Proactive Approach to Isopod Health

In the event of health concerns, having a well-defined first aid protocol is crucial. Isolate affected individuals into a separate enclosure with optimal conditions, providing a stress-free environment for recovery. Consulting with a veterinarian experienced in invertebrate care can offer tailored advice and assistance.

Remedies may include adjustments to environmental parameters, dietary changes, or the use of specialized treatments formulated for isopods. A proactive and well-informed approach to first aid ensures the swift and effective resolution of health issues, safeguarding the health of your entire isopod community.

Chapter 6: Handling and Interaction

As we delve into Chapter 6, the spotlight is on the nuanced art of handling and interacting with isopods. This chapter expands on safe handling practices, explores ways to build a meaningful connection with your isopods, delves into enrichment activities that enhance their well-being, and concludes with the importance of joining communities to share knowledge and experiences.

Safe Handling Practices: A Gentle Approach to Connection

While isopods generally prefer minimal handling, there are instances where interaction becomes necessary for enclosure maintenance, health checks, or the simple joy of connecting with your pets. Adopting safe handling practices is crucial for ensuring the well-being and comfort of your isopod companions.

Gentle Approach: A Symphony of Care

Approach isopods with care and gentleness, recognizing their delicate nature. Sudden movements or disturbances can induce stress, so opting for a slow and deliberate approach allows isopods to acclimate to your presence. This gentle approach establishes trust and minimizes potential stressors during handling.

Moist Hands: Ensuring Respiratory Comfort

Isopods breathe through gills, making the moisture level of your hands paramount during handling. Dry hands can be detrimental to their well-being. Prioritize moist hands to create a more comfortable and less stressful handling experience. A light misting of water on your hands ensures optimal respiratory conditions for your isopods.

Use a Soft Brush: Delicate Handling for Shy Individuals

For more delicate species or individuals prone to stress, consider using a soft brush. This method minimizes direct contact, providing a gentle way to encourage movement without causing undue stress. The soft brush becomes an extension of your care, ensuring the well-being of even the most sensitive isopods.

Bonding with Your Isopods: Observing, Understanding, and Enriching

Building a connection with isopods transcends traditional notions of pet bonding. While they may not respond like mammalian pets, fostering a connection involves observation, environmental enrichment, and an understanding of their unique behaviors.

Quiet Observation: The Art of Patience

Spend time quietly observing your isopods, allowing them to acclimate to your presence and engage in their natural behaviors. Patience is key in building trust over time. By being a patient observer, you gain insights into their individual personalities and social dynamics within the colony.

Environmental Enrichment: Crafting a Dynamic Habitat

Enhance their habitat with elements like rotting wood, leaf litter, and moss. Periodically rearrange the enclosure to stimulate exploration and prevent boredom. A dynamic environment contributes to their mental and physical well-being, fostering a space where natural instincts can be expressed.

Respect Their Space: Individual Personalities in Communal Living

Isopods, with their small and delicate nature, may prefer minimal handling. Respecting their space and allowing them to choose when to interact fosters a stress-free environment. Recognize and appreciate their individual personalities within the communal space. This approach contributes to a harmonious and thriving isopod community.

Enrichment Activities: Elevating Their Isopod Experience

Enrichment is a crucial aspect of keeping any pet, and isopods are no exception. Though their activities may seem subtle, providing elements that mimic their natural habitat enhances their overall well-being.

Natural Materials: Crafting a Microcosm of Nature

Introduce various natural materials into the enclosure, such as rotting wood, dried leaves, and bark. These elements not only serve as hiding places but also provide opportunities for foraging and exploration. Crafting a microcosm of their natural habitat enriches their daily experiences.

Textures and Substrates: Tactile Variety for Sensitive Antennae

Vary the textures within the substrate using materials like coconut coir, sphagnum moss, and sand. Isopods, with their sensitive antennae, will appreciate the tactile variety. This sensory diversity creates a more engaging and stimulating environment.

Rearrangement: Stimulating Mental Engagement

Periodically rearrange the enclosure layout. This simple act provides mental stimulation and encourages isopods to explore their environment. It mimics the dynamic nature of their natural habitats, promoting engagement and preventing monotony.

Joining Isopod Communities: A Shared Passion for Tiny Crustaceans

As we conclude the chapter on handling and interaction, it's essential to recognize the broader community of isopod keepers. Joining communities, sharing knowledge, and participating in events not only enhance your isopod-keeping experience but also contribute to the broader understanding and appreciation of these remarkable crustaceans.

Conclusion: A Symphony of Connection and Community

Handling and interacting with isopods is a delicate dance of care and observation. From safe handling practices to building connections and providing enrichment, this chapter has provided a comprehensive guide to fostering a meaningful relationship with your isopod companions. As you embark on this journey of connection and community, may your bond with these fascinating crustaceans deepen, and your shared experiences contribute to the thriving world of isopod keeping.

Chapter 7: Building a Community of Isopod Keepers

Joining Isopod Enthusiast Communities

Connecting with fellow isopod enthusiasts can transform your solo isopod-keeping journey into a shared adventure. Joining online forums, social media groups, or local clubs dedicated to invertebrate keeping opens the door to a wealth of knowledge, experiences, and camaraderie.

1. **Online Forums and Social Media Groups:** Platforms such as dedicated isopod forums, Reddit communities, and Facebook groups provide virtual spaces to share insights, ask questions, and celebrate the joys and challenges of isopod keeping. Engaging in discussions with members ranging from beginners to seasoned keepers offers diverse perspectives and valuable advice.

2. **Local Clubs and Events:** Explore the possibility of joining local invertebrate or reptile clubs. These gatherings often host events, workshops, and even isopod-specific shows. Connecting with fellow enthusiasts face-to-face fosters a sense of community and may lead to local partnerships, such as trading isopod species or sharing resources.

3. **Collaborative Projects:** Engage in collaborative projects within the community. From breeding challenges to habitat design contests, participating in joint initiatives not only hones your isopod-keeping skills but also strengthens the bonds within the community.

Sharing Knowledge and Experiences

Contributing to the isopod-keeping community by sharing your knowledge and experiences is a rewarding aspect of the journey. It not only enriches the collective understanding of isopod care but also establishes you as an active participant in the community.

1. **Blogs and Journals:** Start a blog or journal chronicling your isopod-keeping experiences. Share your successes, challenges, and any unique observations about your isopod colony. Blogging platforms or dedicated isopod forums provide spaces to document and share your journey.

2. **Social Media Presence:** Utilize social media platforms to share visually engaging content about your isopods. From captivating photos to short videos showcasing their behaviors, social media allows you to connect with a broader audience and contribute to the broader isopod-keeping community.

3. **Workshops and Tutorials:** Consider hosting workshops or tutorials, either online or locally, to share your expertise. Topics could range from habitat setup tips to breeding strategies. Sharing practical knowledge in an accessible format contributes to the collective growth of isopod enthusiasts.

Participating in Isopod Events and Shows

Taking your isopod passion to the next level involves participating in isopod-related events and shows. These gatherings offer a unique platform to meet fellow enthusiasts, learn from experts, and immerse yourself in the diverse world of isopods.

1. **Isopod Shows and Expos:** Attend isopod-specific shows and expos where enthusiasts and breeders come together to showcase their colonies. These events are not only opportunities to acquire new species or morphs but also forums for networking and learning from experienced keepers.

2. **Species Spotlights:** Consider featuring specific isopod species or morphs in collaborative events. This could involve presenting information about a particular species, sharing breeding challenges, or hosting live demonstrations. Such

spotlights contribute to the educational aspect of isopod-keeping.

3. **Educational Outreach:** Volunteer for educational outreach programs, either independently or through established organizations. Introduce isopods to schools, nature centers, or community events to raise awareness and inspire interest in these fascinating creatures.

Chapter 8: Frequently Asked Questions (FAQs)

Q1: What are isopods, and why are they kept as pets?

A1: Isopods are small, terrestrial crustaceans often known as woodlice or pill bugs. They are kept as pets due to their intriguing behaviors, low-maintenance care, and their role in decomposing organic matter, making them beneficial for vivariums and bioactive setups.

Q2: What kind of enclosure is suitable for pet isopods?

A2: Isopods thrive in a variety of enclosures, but a terrarium or vivarium with ample ventilation, substrate for burrowing, and hiding places is ideal. Ensure the enclosure maintains appropriate humidity levels, and consider the specific habitat preferences of your isopod species.

Q3: What do isopods eat, and how often should they be fed?

A3: Isopods are detritivores, primarily feeding on decaying organic matter. Offer a varied diet including leaf litter, rotting wood, and vegetables. Feed them 2-3 times a week, adjusting quantities based on their consumption to avoid overfeeding.

Q4: How do I maintain humidity for my pet isopods?

A4: Use a substrate that retains moisture, mist the enclosure regularly, and provide a shallow water dish. Covering part of the enclosure with a lid or plastic wrap helps maintain humidity, especially for species with higher humidity requirements.

Q5: Can different isopod species be kept together in the same enclosure?

A5: While some isopod species can coexist peacefully, it's generally advisable to keep species separately to avoid competition, potential stress, and ensure their specific habitat needs are met.

Q6: Do isopods require any special lighting?

A6: Isopods are nocturnal and do not require special lighting. Ambient room lighting is usually sufficient. However, ensure a consistent day-night cycle to mimic their natural environment.

Q7: How do I encourage breeding in my isopod colony?

A7: Provide a well-balanced diet, maintain optimal environmental conditions, and ensure a comfortable substrate for breeding and molting. Monitoring population density and avoiding overfeeding can also encourage breeding behaviors.

Q8: What should I do if I notice health issues in my isopods?

A8: Isolate affected individuals, consult a veterinarian experienced in invertebrate care, and consider adjustments to environmental factors or diet. Regular observation, early detection, and a proactive approach to health management are crucial.

Q9: Can isopods escape from their enclosure?

A9: Isopods are generally not skilled climbers, but it's essential to provide a secure lid or barrier to prevent escape. Ensure any ventilation holes are small enough to contain them and regularly check for potential escape points.

Q10: Are there any legal considerations or permits for keeping certain isopod species?

A10: Check local regulations as some isopod species may be subject to restrictions. It's essential to be aware of any permits or legal requirements associated with keeping specific species in your region.

Q11: How long do isopods typically live?

A11: The lifespan of isopods varies among species, but many live for 1-3 years. Proper care, a suitable environment, and a balanced diet contribute to their overall longevity.

Q12: Can isopods be kept as bioactive cleaners in a terrarium?

A12: Yes, isopods are excellent bioactive cleaners, contributing to the breakdown of organic matter, controlling mold, and improving soil structure in vivariums or terrariums. Ensure the isopod species chosen is compatible with the needs of the other inhabitants.

Q13: Can I handle my pet isopods?

A13: Isopods are delicate creatures, and excessive handling can stress them. While occasional gentle handling is generally fine, it's advisable to limit direct contact to minimize stress and potential harm.

Q14: Can isopods transmit diseases to humans or other pets?

A14: Isopods are generally harmless and pose no significant threat to humans or other pets. However, it's essential to practice good hygiene, especially if you have other invertebrates or exotic pets, to prevent cross-contamination.

Q15: Where can I find more information about specific isopod species and their care requirements?

A15: Reputable online forums, isopod enthusiast communities, and scientific literature are valuable resources. Additionally, consult care sheets provided by reputable breeders or suppliers for species-specific information.

Q16: Can isopods be kept with other invertebrates or small reptiles?

A16: While isopods are generally compatible with small reptiles like geckos or invertebrates in a bioactive setup, compatibility depends on the specific species and their individual needs. Always research and monitor interactions to ensure the well-being of all inhabitants.

Q17: How do I prevent mold growth in the isopod enclosure?

A17: Mold growth can be minimized by maintaining proper ventilation, avoiding overfeeding, and ensuring that the substrate doesn't become overly saturated. Regularly remove uneaten food and decaying matter to prevent mold proliferation.

Q18: Are there any considerations for isopod hibernation?

A18: Some temperate isopod species may benefit from a period of cooler temperatures to simulate winter conditions. Research the specific hibernation requirements of your isopod species and adjust environmental conditions accordingly.

Q19: What are signs of stress in isopods, and how can I alleviate it?

A19: Signs of stress may include decreased activity, changes in color, or excessive hiding. To alleviate stress, ensure a stable environment, provide hiding places, and minimize disturbances. Evaluate and adjust environmental factors if needed.

Q20: Can isopods be kept in a bioactive aquarium or paludarium?

A20: Isopods can thrive in bioactive setups, contributing to the ecosystem's balance. Ensure proper substrate, humidity, and hiding spaces, and research compatibility with aquatic elements for paludariums.

Q21: Can isopods live solely on a commercial isopod food diet?

A21: While commercial isopod food can be a convenient supplement, a varied diet mimicking their natural environment is essential for long-term health. Include leaf litter, decomposing wood, and vegetables for optimal nutrition.

Q22: How do I manage isopod population control?

A22: Regularly monitor population density, adjust feeding amounts, and provide suitable hiding places for young isopods. If needed, consider relocating excess individuals to another enclosure or sharing them with fellow hobbyists.

Q23: Can I use wild-caught isopods as pets?

A23: While it's possible, using wild-caught isopods carries risks, including potential exposure to pesticides or diseases. It's generally recommended to start with captive-bred isopods from reputable sources to ensure a healthy and disease-free population.

Q24: How do I create a suitable isopod habitat for a specific species?

A24: Research the natural habitat, substrate preferences, and environmental conditions of the specific isopod species. Mimic these conditions in the enclosure, providing suitable hiding spots and maintaining the correct temperature and humidity.

Q25: Can I breed isopods intentionally, and how do I promote breeding behavior?

A25: Yes, intentional breeding is possible. To promote breeding, provide a balanced diet, optimal environmental conditions, and ensure suitable hiding spots for molting and reproduction. Monitor population density and adjust feeding accordingly.

Q26: What is the lifespan of isopod eggs, and how can I care for the young?

A26: Isopod egg incubation periods vary, but on average, it takes several weeks. Provide a humid environment for hatching and offer small, soft foods for the young isopods. Monitor humidity levels to prevent desiccation.

Q27: Can isopods be kept outdoors in certain climates?

A27: In temperate climates, some isopod species can be kept outdoors, especially in bioactive gardens. Ensure they are native to the region or have similar climate requirements, and provide suitable hiding places.

Q28: How do I acclimate newly acquired isopods to their enclosure?

A28: Gradually introduce new isopods to their enclosure to allow them to acclimate. Start with a small group, monitor their behavior, and avoid sudden changes to environmental conditions to minimize stress.

Q29: Are there any potential hazards for isopods in the home environment?

A29: Ensure that cleaning products, pesticides, or other chemicals are kept away from isopod enclosures. Additionally, be cautious of household pets that may view isopods as prey. Always practice good hygiene to prevent contamination.

Q30: What can I do if my isopods are not molting successfully?

A30: Evaluate the environmental conditions, ensuring proper humidity and calcium availability. Adjust the diet to include calcium-rich foods, and consider consulting a veterinarian for guidance on promoting successful molting in isopods.

Appendix

Glossary of Isopod Terminology

Embark on a journey through the intricate lexicon of isopod keeping with confidence, using this expansive glossary as your compass. From fundamental biological terms to habitat-specific jargon, this section aims to not only provide definitions but to offer detailed explanations, enriching your comprehension of isopod biology and care.

1. Molt: Unveiling the Art of Exoskeletal Transformation

Molt Process: A Symphony of Growth

Molting is a pivotal aspect of the isopod life cycle, representing the remarkable process of shedding the exoskeleton to accommodate growth. This section delves into the intricacies of molting, elucidating the stages involved and the physiological changes that transpire. Understanding the molt process is fundamental for isopod keepers as it directly impacts the well-being and vitality of these crustaceans.

Frequency and Significance: Unraveling the Molting Mystery

This subsection explores the frequency of molting in isopods, shedding light on the factors that influence molting frequency, such as age, species, and environmental conditions. Delving into the significance of molting unveils its role not only in growth but also in regenerating damaged body parts and aiding in reproduction. By comprehending the molting intricacies, you gain a deeper insight into the dynamic nature of isopod biology.

2. Bioactive: Crafting Ecosystems within Enclosures

Definition: An Ecosystem in Miniature

The term "bioactive" takes center stage in the isopod keeping lexicon, describing an enclosure that transcends the conventional by incorporating living organisms. In this section, explore the depth of bioactivity, where isopods play a crucial role in contributing to natural decomposition and waste breakdown. The bioactive approach transforms isopod enclosures into dynamic ecosystems, fostering a self-sustaining balance that mimics nature.

Isopods as Decomposers: Environmental Stewards in Action

Unveiling the role of isopods as decomposers, this subsection details how they actively participate in the breakdown of organic matter within the enclosure. By assimilating their waste breakdown activities, isopods become environmental stewards, influencing nutrient cycling and contributing to the overall health of the habitat. Understanding the bioactive concept provides keepers with a holistic approach to enclosure management.

3. Morph: Exploring the Kaleidoscope of Isopod Variation

Defining Morph: Beyond Species Uniformity

Within a single species, diversity manifests through morphs, distinct variations characterized by specific coloration, patterns, or traits. This section navigates the spectrum of isopod morphology, exploring the genetic and environmental factors that influence morph development. From striking color variations to unique patterns, uncover the fascinating world of morphs that adds an extra layer of intrigue to isopod keeping.

Genetic Basis and Selective Breeding: Shaping Isopod Aesthetics

Delving into the genetic foundation of morphs, this subsection elucidates how selective breeding practices can influence and enhance specific traits within isopod populations. Keepers seeking to cultivate unique morphs can employ selective breeding strategies, contributing to the aesthetic diversity within the isopod community. Understanding morphs and their genetic underpinnings enhances appreciation for the diversity encapsulated within a single species.

4. Sow Bug vs. Pill Bug: Navigating Isopod Nomenclature

Terminology Demystified: Clarifying Common Names

Isopods are often referred to as sow bugs or pill bugs, but what's the difference? This section demystifies the common names, providing clarity on the distinction between sow bugs and pill bugs. Understanding the nomenclature ensures accurate communication among isopod enthusiasts and prevents confusion surrounding the diverse isopod species.

Habitat and Behavior: Exploring Sow Bug and Pill Bug Lifestyles

Delving into the habitat preferences and behavior of sow bugs and pill bugs, this subsection sheds light on the subtle differences that contribute to their distinct identities. Whether it's the shape of the body or habitat choices, each nuance adds to the rich tapestry of isopod diversity. By understanding the intricacies of sow bugs and pill bugs, keepers can tailor their care practices to accommodate the specific needs of these fascinating crustaceans.

5. Armadillidium vs. Porcellio: Navigating Isopod Genera

Genera Defined: Unraveling the Diversity of Isopod Families

Isopods belong to different genera, with Armadillidium and Porcellio being among the most well-known. In this section, explore the defining characteristics that distinguish Armadillidium and Porcellio, gaining insights into their biology, behavior, and preferred habitats. Navigating the nuances of isopod genera enhances your ability to provide species-specific care tailored to Armadillidium or Porcellio colonies.

Preferred Environments: Tailoring Care to Genera-Specific Needs

Uncover the preferred environments that Armadillidium and Porcellio thrive in, from substrate choices to humidity levels. Understanding the specific needs of each genus empowers keepers to create environments that cater to the well-being and natural behaviors of these isopod communities. By tailoring care practices to genera-specific requirements, keepers contribute to the flourishing health of their isopod colonies.

6. Parthenogenesis: A Marvel of Asexual Reproduction

Parthenogenesis Defined: A Reproductive Marvel

Parthenogenesis, the process of asexual reproduction, takes center stage in this section. Unravel the marvel of parthenogenesis, where females can produce offspring without fertilization. This subsection explores the mechanisms behind parthenogenesis, its prevalence in certain isopod species, and the implications for isopod populations. Understanding parthenogenesis adds a fascinating layer to the reproductive strategies of these resilient crustaceans.

Advantages and Limitations: Navigating the Parthenogenetic Path

Delving into the advantages and limitations of parthenogenesis, this subsection elucidates how this reproductive strategy influences isopod populations. While parthenogenesis offers advantages in rapid population growth, it also comes with inherent limitations that impact genetic diversity. Exploring the intricacies of parthenogenesis enhances your grasp of isopod reproductive dynamics and the evolutionary strategies employed by different species.

7. Isopod Anatomy: A Comprehensive Exploration

Exoskeleton Structure: Armor of Resilience

Navigate the intricacies of isopod anatomy in this section, focusing on the exoskeleton as a defining feature. Explore the composition and structure of the exoskeleton, understanding its role as a protective armor for isopods. This subsection delves into the exoskeletal growth process, molting cycles, and the significance of a well-formed exoskeleton in ensuring the survival and resilience of isopod individuals.

Antennae and Sensory Perception: Navigating the World through Antennae

Isopods rely on antennae for sensory perception, communication, and navigation of their environment. This subsection unravels the significance of antennae, exploring their structure, function, and role in isopod behavior. Understanding how isopods perceive their surroundings through antennae enhances your

Pet Isopods Setup Checklist: Getting Started on Isopod Keeping

Starting with pet isopods requires careful preparation to ensure a healthy and thriving environment for these fascinating crustaceans. Here's a comprehensive checklist to guide you in setting up a successful isopod habitat:

1. Enclosure:

- Appropriate-sized enclosure with secure, well-ventilated lid.
- Consider bioactive setups with live plants for added ecological balance.

2. Substrate:

- Coconut coir, sphagnum moss, or a mix of soil and leaf litter for the substrate.
- Ensure substrate depth for burrowing and hiding places.

3. Humidity and Moisture:

- Mist bottle for maintaining humidity levels.
- Water dish or dampened sphagnum moss for hydration.

4. Hideouts:

- Cork bark, rotting wood, or other natural materials for isopods to hide under.

- Provide ample hiding places to reduce stress.

5. Temperature:

- Thermometer to monitor temperature, keeping it within the suitable range for the chosen isopod species.

6. Lighting:

- Low-wattage, indirect lighting for visibility (isopods are nocturnal).

- Live plants can benefit from proper lighting.

7. Ventilation:

- Ensure proper ventilation to prevent excess moisture buildup.

- Ventilation holes or mesh on the sides or lid of the enclosure.

8. Food and Nutrition:

- Variety of leaf litter (oak, maple, etc.) for natural foraging.

- Vegetables (carrots, zucchini, cucumber) for a balanced diet.

- Calcium source (crushed eggshells, cuttlebone) for exoskeleton health.

- Commercial isopod food as a supplement.

9. Cleanup Crew:

- Consider adding springtails as a cleanup crew to assist in waste decomposition.

- Assess the compatibility of isopods with other invertebrates if planning a mixed bioactive setup.

10. Monitoring Tools:

- Hygrometer to measure humidity levels.

- pH testing strips for substrate assessment.

- Keep a logbook to record observations and any changes in the enclosure.

11. Handling Supplies:

- Soft paintbrush or a small, soft brush for gently handling isopods.

- Avoid handling isopods excessively to reduce stress.

12. Research:

- Thoroughly research the specific requirements of the isopod species you plan to keep.

- Understand their natural habitat, behavior, and breeding patterns.

13. Quarantine Setup:

- If acquiring isopods from different sources, set up a quarantine enclosure to observe and ensure they are healthy before introducing them to the main habitat.

14. Veterinarian Contact:

- Have contact information for a veterinarian experienced in invertebrate care.

- Be prepared with basic first aid supplies for isopod health concerns.

15. Education:

- Stay informed about isopod care through reputable sources and community forums.

- Be open to learning and adapting your setup based on your observations.

By diligently preparing and checking off each item on this list, you'll be well-equipped to create a suitable and enriching environment for your pet isopods. Regular observation, attention to detail, and a genuine interest in their well-being will contribute to a rewarding experience in the world of isopod keeping.

Made in United States
Troutdale, OR
05/19/2024

19987254R00040